Relationships of Living Things

AUTHORS

Mary Atwater
The University of Georgia

Prentice Baptiste
University of Houston

Lucy Daniel
Rutherford County Schools

Jay Hackett
University of Northern Colorado

Richard Moyer
University of Michigan, Dearborn

Carol Takemoto
Los Angeles Unified School District

Nancy Wilson
Sacramento Unified School District

Macmillan/McGraw-Hill School Publishing Company
New York   Chicago   Columbus

MACMILLAN / McGRAW-HILL

SCIENCE TURNS MINDS ON™

CONSULTANTS

Assessment:
Janice M. Camplin
Curriculum Coordinator, Elementary Science
Mentor, Western New York
Lake Shore Central Schools
Angola, NY

Mary Hamm
Associate Professor
Department of Elementary Education
San Francisco State University
San Francisco, CA

Cognitive Development:
Dr. Elisabeth Charron
Assistant Professor of Science Education
Montana State University
Bozeman, MT

Sue Teele
Director of Education Extension
University of California, Riverside
Riverside, CA

Cooperative Learning:
Harold Pratt
Executive Director of Curriculum
Jefferson County Public Schools
Golden, CO

Earth Science:
Thomas A. Davies
Research Scientist
The University of Texas
Austin, TX

David G. Futch
Associate Professor of Biology
San Diego State University
San Diego, CA

Dr. Shadia Rifai Habbal
Harvard-Smithsonian Center for Astrophysics
Cambridge, MA

Tom Murphree, Ph.D.
Global Systems Studies
Monterey, CA

Suzanne O'Connell
Assistant Professor
Wesleyan University
Middletown, CT

Environmental Education:
Cheryl Charles, Ph.D.
Executive Director
Project Wild
Boulder, CO

Gifted:
Sandra N. Kaplan
Associate Director, National/State Leadership
Training Institute on the Gifted/Talented
Ventura County Superintendent of Schools Office
Northridge, CA

Global Education:
M. Eugene Gilliom
Professor of Social Studies and Global Education
The Ohio State University
Columbus, OH

Merry M. Merryfield
Assistant Professor of Social Studies and Global
Education
The Ohio State University
Columbus, OH

Intermediate Specialist
Sharon L. Strating
Missouri State Teacher of the Year
Northwest Missouri State University
Marysville, MO

Life Science:
Carl D. Barrentine
Associate Professor of Biology
California State University
Bakersfield, CA

V.L. Holland
Professor and Chair, Biological Sciences
Department
California Polytechnic State University
San Luis Obispo, CA

Donald C. Lisowy
Education Specialist
New York, NY

Dan B. Walker
Associate Dean for Science Education and
Professor of Biology
San Jose State University
San Jose, CA

Literature:
Dr. Donna E. Norton
Texas A&M University
College Station, TX

Tina Thoburn, Ed.D.
President
Thoburn Educational Enterprises, Inc.
Ligonier, PA

Copyright © 1993 Macmillan/McGraw-Hill School Publishing Company

Macmillan/McGraw-Hill School Division
10 Union Square East
New York, New York 10003

Printed in the United States of America

ISBN 0-02-274264-6 / 3

3 4 5 6 7 8 9 VHJ 99 98 97 96 95 94 93

Shallow reef in Red Sea

Mathematics:

Martin L. Johnson
Professor, Mathematics Education
University of Maryland at College Park
College Park, MD

Physical Science:

Max Diem, Ph.D.
Professor of Chemistry
City University of New York, Hunter College
New York, NY

Gretchen M. Gillis
Geologist
Maxus Exploration Company
Dallas, TX

Wendell H. Potter
Associate Professor of Physics
Department of Physics
University of California, Davis
Davis, CA

Claudia K. Viehland
Educational Consultant, Chemist
Sigma Chemical Company
St. Louis, MO

Reading:

Jean Wallace Gillet
Reading Teacher
Charlottesville Public Schools
Charlottesville, VA

Charles Temple, Ph. D.
Associate Professor of Education
Hobart and William Smith Colleges
Geneva, NY

Safety:

Janice Sutkus
Program Manager: Education

National Safety Council
Chicago, IL

Science Technology and Society (STS):

William C. Kyle, Jr.
Director, School Mathematics and Science Center
Purdue University
West Lafayette, IN

Social Studies:

Mary A. McFarland
Instructional Coordinator of
Social Studies, K-12, and
Director of Staff Development
Parkway School District
St. Louis, MO

Students Acquiring English:

Mrs. Bronwyn G. Frederick, M.A.
Bilingual Teacher
Pomona Unified School District
Pomona, CA

Misconceptions:

Dr. Charles W. Anderson
Michigan State University
East Lansing, MI

Dr. Edward L. Smith
Michigan State University
East Lansing, MI

Multicultural:

Bernard L. Charles
Senior Vice President
Quality Education for Minorities Network
Washington, DC

Cheryl Willis Hudson
Graphic Designer and Publishing Consultant
Part Owner and Publisher, Just Us Books, Inc.
Orange, NJ

Paul B. Janeczko
Poet
Hebron, MA

James R. Murphy
Math Teacher
La Guardia High School
New York, NY

Ramon L. Santiago
Professor of Education and Director of ESL
Lehman College, City University of New York
Bronx, NY

Clifford E. Trafzer
Professor and Chair, Ethnic Studies
University of California, Riverside
Riverside, CA

STUDENT ACTIVITY TESTERS

Jennifer Kildow
Brooke Straub
Cassie Zistl
Betsy McKeown
Seth McLaughlin
Max Berry
Wayne Henderson

FIELD TEST TEACHERS

Sharon Ervin
San Pablo Elementary School
Jacksonville, FL

Michelle Gallaway
Indianapolis Public School #44
Indianapolis, IN

Kathryn Gallman
#7 School
Rochester, NY

Karla McBride
#44 School
Rochester, NY

Diane Pease
Leopold Elementary
Madison, WI

Kathy Perez
Martin Luther King Elementary
Jacksonville, FL

Ralph Stamler
Thoreau School
Madison, WI

Joanne Stern
Hilltop Elementary School
Glen Burnie, MD

Janet Young
Indianapolis Public School #90
Indianapolis, IN

CONTRIBUTING WRITER

Linda Barr

Relationships of Living Things

Lessons   **Themes**

Activities!

EXPLORE

TRY THIS

Features

 Links

Departments

Relationships of Living Things

If you could visit any place on Earth, where would you go? Would you explore the rain forests of Tanzania? Would you climb mountains in Chile (chil´ē)? How about going to the outback in Australia? Perhaps you'd like to see a bustling city like Tokyo (tō´ kyō). Maybe you'd choose the desert stillness of the American Southwest. What about an adventurous trip to the South Pole? There are so many fascinating places on Earth. Where would you like to go?

Which of these places is closest to where you live?
Which one is the farthest away?

Torres del Paine National Park, Chile

Mitre Rock, Victoria Australia

Tokyo, Japan

Whatever place you choose, in some ways it is like the place where you live. Everywhere on Earth, many different kinds of living things share the same space. In this unit you'll find out how living things affect each other. You'll also find out what happens when we don't take care of the spaces we share.

Dunes near Riyadh, Saudi Arabia

In what ways is this desert like the place where you live? In what ways is it different?

Minds On! On page 1 in your ***Activity Log,*** make a list of the living things that share your neighborhood with you. ●

Sights and Sounds

Tour guides know all the wonderful things to see and do in the places where they live. They know all about the weather, places of natural beauty, festivals, and history. It's their job to share what they know with visitors. Look at the pictures on these pages. What do you think a tour guide might tell people about these places? If you enjoy people and like to share what you learn, this may be the job for you!

A shallow reef in the Red Sea

In the water, as well as on land, living things share the same space. What kinds of living things, besides fish, live in water?

9

Science in Literature

These books will take you to many different places. One will take you to a different time. In all of them, you'll find different kinds of living things sharing the same space.

Very Last First Time by Jan Andrews.
New York: Atheneum, 1985.

This book takes you to an Inuit (in´ü it) village on Ungava Bay in Northern Canada. You'll take a walk on the bottom of the sea in winter while the tide is out. It's an experience you won't forget.

As you read, notice that you get information in two ways. Both the words and the pictures tell the story. Compare what you learn from the words and pictures. Write your thoughts on page 2 of your **Activity Log.** Share your ideas with another student.

VERY LAST FIRST TIME
BY Jan Andrews ILLUSTRATED BY Ian Wallace

Urban Roosts
by Barbara Bash.
Boston: Little, Brown and
Company, 1990.

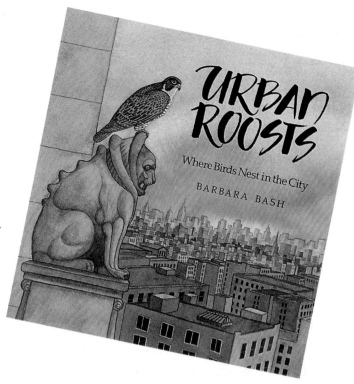

If you live in a city, this
book may really open your
eyes. Birds have found some
surprising places to live.
Many of them are right under
your nose, or over your head,
or even in your house!
Whether you notice it or not,
you are sharing your space.

Other Good Books To Read

The Roadside
by David Bellamy.
New York: Clarkson N. Potter, Inc.,
1988.
This book shows what happens
to animals when a road is built
through the place where they
live. It will help you see how
what humans do affects other
living things.

Just a Dream
by Chris Van Allsburg.
Boston: Houghton Mifflin, 1990.
A young boy dreams about a
future Earth badly damaged by
pollution.

The Great Kapok Tree: A
Tale of the Amazon
Rain Forest
by Lynne Cherry.
New York: Harcourt, Brace,
Jovanovich, 1990.
In this modern fable, the animals
of a rain forest persuade a man
not to cut down a tree that is an
important part of their space.

Living Together

Living things have needs. They stay in places where they can get food and minerals (min´ər əlz), water, air, shelter, space, and the right temperature. Some animals need to live in cold places. You need to live where you can stay warm. In this lesson, you'll learn more about the ways living things— like you—depend on other living things and on things that are not living.

Polar bears live along the northern coasts of Canada, Greenland, Alaska, and Russia. They also live on islands in the Arctic Ocean. What would you need to be comfortable in a polar bear's ecosystem?

Polar bears need food such as seals, sea birds, and fish. They also need lots of space. A layer of fat under their thick fur keeps them warm.

Why wouldn't a desert be the best ecosystem for a polar bear? How about under some leaves in a forest? What about in the ocean?

Minds On! Do you know what an ecosystem (ek´ō sis´təm) is? Look above for some clues. On page 3 in your *Activity Log,* list seven places you think are ecosystems. In the next activity, you'll find out more by exploring one. ●

Activity!

What Is in an Ecosystem?

An ecosystem can be as small as a decaying log or as large as an ocean. What are the parts that make up an ecosystem? In this activity you will be studying a small ecosystem to find out.

What You Need

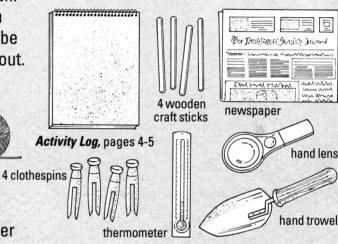

meter tape

ball of yarn

Activity Log, pages 4-5

4 wooden craft sticks

newspaper

hand lens

4 clothespins

thermometer

hand trowel

What To Do

1 Choose a natural area to study. Mark off an area that is one meter square. Stick a clothespin into the ground at each corner. Wrap yarn around the tops of the clothespins to make the square.

2 Look carefully for plants and animals inside the square. Try not to disturb the area you are observing. Use the craft sticks to look between the plants. Look for signs of animals, such as a hole dug in the ground or prints. Record the number and kind of each organism (ôr′ gə niz′ əm) that you see.

3 Use the hand trowel to dig up some of the topsoil. Spread it on the newspaper. Use the hand lens to observe the topsoil. Record any organisms that you see.

4 Draw a picture of the living things in the area. Show plants, insects, and other living things.

5 Measure and record the temperature at ground level.

6 Record the nonliving things in the area. Describe the color and texture of the soil.

What Happened?

1. How many different kinds of nonliving things did you have in your ecosystem? What nonliving thing did you have the most of?

2. How many different kinds of living things did you have in your ecosystem? What living thing did you have the most of?

3. Is anything in your ecosystem eating something else? How can you tell?

What Now?

1. What other things might live in the ecosystem you observed?

2. Could you live in this ecosystem? Could a polar bear? Why?

EXPLORE

Large and Small Ecosystems

The area you just studied had living and nonliving things. There may have been plants and animals such as insects, worms, and spiders. Other organisms live there, too. But they are too small to see. The nonliving things might have included air, water, rocks, soil, and sunlight.

Organisms depend on both the living and the nonliving things around them. Plants, insects, and other animals depend on air, water, and sunlight to stay alive. The animals might also eat the plants. They might use the plants, rocks, and soil for shelter.

What do you think would happen here if the plants all died? What would happen if the sun stopped shining on it? What would happen if you added something?

TRY THIS

Activity!

Something Added

Return to the ecosystem that you observed in the Explore Activity. Work with the same group you worked with before.

What You Need

piece of bread, fruit, or vegetable; *Activity Log* page 6

Add the food to the area, and observe how the ecosystem changes over a week. Record your observations. Compare the changes with those seen by other groups.

Groups of living things interacting with each other and the place where they live make up an **ecosystem.** The person who studies an ecosystem decides on its size. What was the size of the one you studied?

Earth may be thought of as one large ecosystem.

Desert near Tucson, Arizona

Earth contains smaller ecosystems, such as forests, deserts, towns, and cities.

Pool in Alamo Canyon, Arizona

These ecosystems contain still smaller ones, such as a canyon, a stream, a dead log, a puddle, or even the area under a rock.

A Swamp Ecosystem

All the living things in a certain area—animals, plants, fungi (fun´jī), bacteria (bak tîr´ē ə), and other organisms—make up a **community**. What are some different kinds of living things in your own community?

A group of organisms of the same kind living in the same area at the same time is called a **population** (pop´ yə lā´ shən). What are some of the different populations in this swamp community?

The organisms in a population live together because they have the same needs.

Cypress and Spanish moss

Cypress tree

Pileated woodpecker

Green darner

Skunk cabbage

Pitcher plant

Sword fern

American alligator

Florida cottonmouth

Fowler's toad

Muskrat

Golden club

Golden orb spider

Wild iris

The place in an ecosystem where a population lives and grows is called a **habitat** (hab´i tat´). Each population in a swamp lives in a habitat that meets its needs.

Minds On! Think about your habitat. On page 7 in your *Activity Log,* list five things you need to live and grow. Beside each, tell where or how you get it. ●

18

Florida red-bellied turtle

Often, several populations share the same habitat. What populations live in the water? Which ones live in the soil? Which live on the ground?

Gray Squirrel

Anhinga

The habitat of one population may be on or in another population. A tree can be a bird's habitat. That same tree can also be the habitat of vines, a squirrel, and many insects.

White tail deer

Wild grape vine

Yellow butterwort

Florida puma

Great egret

Cattail

Green tree frog

Water lily

Eastern box turtle

TRY THIS **Activity!** *Under a Stone*

What lives in the habitat beneath a stone?

What You Need

small stone or piece of wet cardboard that has been lying on the ground, *Activity Log* **page 8**

What populations do you think would live in this habitat? Record your predictions. Now carefully lift up the stone. Record your observations. Then be sure to put the stone back in place. Remember, it's a home for living things. If you don't put it back, you could destroy the habitat. If you looked under a stone somewhere else, would you expect to find the same kinds of populations? Why or why not?

Whose Habitat?

You are part of an ecosystem of living and nonliving things. The living things—people, pets, birds, insects, trees, bushes, flowers, and grass—make up a community. You are part of one population in your community. The polar bear is part of one population in its community of living things in the Arctic. Your habitat provides the food, water, shelter, and space you need to live and grow.

Minds On! Look at the ecosystems you listed on page 3 of your ***Activity Log.*** Did you name places like forests, fields, streams, and deserts? Did you also list smaller ecosystems, like a puddle or a log? Compare your list with a classmate's list. Did you name any of the same ecosystems?●

Your habitat didn't always look the way it does now, especially if you live in a town or city. Once it was the home of many different populations.

Housing development in Marin County, California

Then things began to change. The forests were cut down to build houses and roads. Meadows became back yards, and streams and ponds were filled in with soil.

Mule deer

Brown bear

Mountain lion

Marsh hawk

Aquilegia plants

Animals like bears, mountain lions, wolves, and hawks left for habitats with fewer people.

Wildflowers died. Their original habitats no longer provided the food, water, shelter, and living space these organisms needed.

When habitats change, the entire ecosystem changes. When you hear about a kind of plant or animal becoming **endangered** (en dān´ jərd), it is usually because there is no longer enough suitable habitat. Some of these plants and animals are now extinct. **Extinct** (ek stingkt´) means there are no more of them still alive. Do you know of any plants or animals that are endangered or extinct?

They're Back!

When the habitat changes, plants don't have any choice. They either survive where they are or they die. Animals do have a choice. They can leave or they can stay.

Many animals are driven away as their habitats become towns and cities. Others have learned how to live with people.

Opossums and raccoons live in attics and find food in garbage cans, not forests.

Moose eat bushes around houses from Maine to Alaska.

Falcons nest on the rooftops of tall buildings in cities in the same way they used to nest on mountain cliffs.

Many areas now have programs to provide new or improved habitats for animals that have lost their natural homes. Protecting habitats is an important way to keep animals and plants from becoming extinct. Are there any of these programs where you live?

Literature Link   *Urban Roosts*

In *Urban Roosts* by Barbara Bash, you'll find out where birds live in the city. They build nests in places you'd never think to look. After you've read the book, walk through your neighborhood or an area near your school. Compare what you see with what you found in the book. Record your observations on page 9 in your **Activity Log.** Then share them with your class.

Rock dove with nest in sign

Minds On! Imagine a habitat that could be set up on an empty lot in your neighborhood. Draw a picture of it on page 10 in your **Activity Log.** Remember to include plants and animals in your habitat. ●

Sum It Up

What smaller word do you see in *ecosystem?* You know that a *system* is a group of things that work together. In an ecosystem the living things interact with each other and with the nonliving things, too. That's how an ecosystem works.

Critical Thinking

1. What are some living and nonliving things in your ecosystem?

2. How do people make it harder for plants and animals to live in your community?

3. How could people make it easier for plants and animals to live in your community?

Getting Food

Earth is a carefully balanced system. In a way, it's like a watch. It has many parts that must all work together. It needs energy to keep it running. In this lesson you'll find out where that energy comes from. You'll also find out what happens to it as it flows through the system.

Did you drink some milk today? Food like milk gives you energy to work and play. Your milk came from cows, which eat grass and other plants to get the energy they need. The grass gets energy from the sun. Did you know your glass of milk depends on the sun?

Holstein cows

Minds On! One more thing about milk—
after a while, it gets sour. Why
does that happen? Write what you think on
page 11 in your *Activity Log.* ●

In the next activity, you'll find out more
about how energy flows through Earth's
system.

Activity!

How Does the Energy Move?

Suppose you left your lunch box at school over the weekend. You know the food won't look the same on Monday as it did on Friday. What happened to it? And what does what happened have to do with energy moving through Earth's system?

What You Need

Activity Log, pages 12-13

2 small pieces of apple

2 small pieces of cheese

2 small pieces of bread

6 zip-lip plastic bags

water

dropper

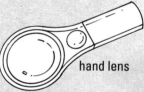
hand lens

What To Do

1 Working with a partner, fill the dropper with water. Moisten each food sample. Wait five minutes.

2 Observe each sample. Record your observations.

Safety!

See the *Safety Tip* in step 5.

3 Place each sample in one of the bags and seal the bag.

4 Put three of the bags (one of each kind of food) in a warm, dark place. Put the other three bags in a refrigerator. Predict what you think will happen to each set of samples. Record your predictions.

5 Observe the bags every day for the next four days. *Safety Tip:* Do not open the bags. Use a hand lens to examine the food inside each bag. Record your observations.

What Happened?

1. Compare the samples kept in a warm, dark place with the ones kept in the refrigerator. How are they the same? How are they different?

2. On which samples did organisms appear? How long did it take?

3. What are the organisms doing to the food?

What Now?

1. Think about your observations. What do you think would happen if you took the samples out of the refrigerator and put them in a warm, dark place for a week?

2. What kind of environment do these organisms prefer?

3. How do these organisms get the energy they need?

EXPLORE

Energy in the Ecosystem

In the Explore Activity, mold grew on the samples that weren't in the refrigerator. Mold is a living thing. It's a fungus (fung´ gəs) that sometimes looks fuzzy and can be different colors. Molds get food by breaking down the substances they grow on. Mold is too small to see until it begins to grow. It grows faster in warm, dark places than in cold ones. Molds and other living things like them are part of how energy flows through an ecosystem.

Green plants are called **producers** (prə dū´ sərz) because they use the sun's energy, along with other substances, to make their own food.

Animals can't make their own food. They are called **consumers** (kən sü´mərz) because they use plants or other consumers to get energy.

Consumers eat many, many producers or other consumers to replace the energy they use. A growing consumer (like you) needs lots of energy to grow new cells.

28

Energy from food keeps plant cells alive. Plants store food they don't need in roots, stems, leaves, and flowers.

Mold on orange

Bacteria

Some consumers are decomposers. **Decomposers** (dē´ kəm pō´ zərz) get energy by causing dead organisms to decay.

Fungi, such as mold, and some bacteria and worms are decomposers.

Other consumers are scavengers. **Scavengers** (skav´ ən jərz), such as vultures, crabs, and crows, get their energy by eating dead organisms.

Sometimes these consumers work together to get rid of dead organisms. After scavengers finish eating, decomposers break down what's left.

You may have seen scavengers eating animals killed on a highway.

Lappet-faced vultures

Activity!

A Worm Box

Remember the sour milk you wrote about on page 11 of your *Activity Log?* Bacterial decomposers changed the milk to get the energy they needed. In this activity you'll see some different decomposers at work. They will help you make some compost. **Compost** (kom´ pōst) is a mixture of decaying plant materials that makes soil richer and more fertile.

What You Need

shoe box, wooden spoon, lettuce leaf, potato peeling, newspaper, water, dry leaves, soil, 6 earthworms, *Activity Log* **page 14**

Tear up some newspaper into 20 small pieces. Moisten the pieces, and put them into the box. Sprinkle in a few crumbled up leaves. Fill the box 2/3 full with soil. Break the lettuce leaf and potato peeling into small pieces, and add them to the box. Last, put in the worms. Keep the box moist, adding a cup of water twice a week. **Carefully** turn the soil over. Record your observations. After three weeks mix the compost into the soil around plants. Release the worms into a safe environment. What did you learn from your observations?

Keep It Moving

The energy in ecosystems flows from the sun to producers to consumers in a food chain. In a **food chain,** each living thing may be food for the next living thing.

The arrows show how the energy is moving.

Follow the arrows to see the beginning and end of each food chain. How many food chains are there?

What else might the hawk eat from another food chain?

Overlapping food chains are called a **food web.** What else might the fox eat from another food chain?

What happens to energy as it moves through food chains and food webs?

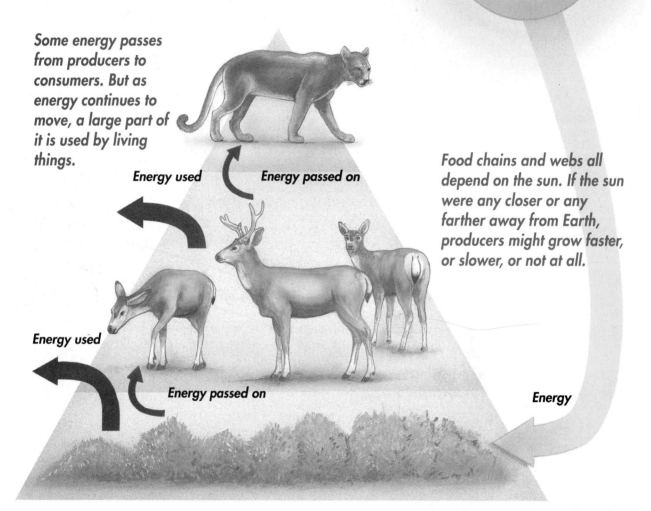

Some energy passes from producers to consumers. But as energy continues to move, a large part of it is used by living things.

Energy used

Energy passed on

Energy used

Energy passed on

Food chains and webs all depend on the sun. If the sun were any closer or any farther away from Earth, producers might grow faster, or slower, or not at all.

Energy

A change in the number of producers would affect all the food chains and webs—every living thing on Earth, including you!

Minds On! On page 15 in your *Activity Log,* draw a food chain that begins with a producer and ends with you. Compare your food chain with those of three classmates. Do you all have the same living things and the same number of steps?●

Seeing the Connections

Have you ever had uninvited picnic guests? Even though ants, mosquitoes, and other insects can be pests, they're an important link in the food chain. If they were all suddenly killed, fish and birds would soon die, too. They wouldn't have enough food. And people who eat birds and fish would have to find something else to eat.

Minds On! Suppose all the plants in a forest ecosystem died. What difference would that make to foxes and snakes? They don't eat plants. Write what you think on page 15 of your *Activity Log.*●

Language Arts Link

It's a Riddle!

Choose a plant and an animal that you like. On page 16 in your *Activity Log,* write a riddle about each one. Put clues about its habitat, what it eats, and what might eat it. Share your riddles with your class. See if they can guess the answers.

Web of Death

One food web stretched from California to the Arctic—and carried DDT with it. DDT is a chemical that was used to kill insects.

DDT was sprayed on crops.

Runoff carried it to the ocean where it settled on small plants that fish ate.

White mullet

When the fish swam north, seals ate many of them.

Pelicans ate the fish, too. The DDT caused them to lay eggs with thin shells. Many eggs were crushed. DDT in their food chain nearly wiped out the pelicans.

Polar bears ate large numbers of seals. As the amount of DDT in their bodies increased, many bears died.

Because it's so dangerous, DDT isn't used much any more in the United States.

Insects can be controlled in other ways. The Chinese were among the first to find natural ways to do this. Around A.D. 100 they discovered a powder made from chrysanthemum (krə san´ thə məm) flowers that kills certain insects but is not harmful to other organisms.

 **Focus on Environment**

Instant Worms!

Scientists know that some of the tiny worms called nematodes (nem´ə tōdz) kill insects without harming other organisms. Now they can ship the worms to farmers who need them. They put live worms into a liquid that pulls water from their bodies. Then the dried worms are refrigerated and shipped. When farmers add water, the worms plump back up. They're good as new and hungry for insects that eat up crops! Do you think this is a good way to control insects? Why?

Sum It Up

You and other living things on Earth depend on the sun for energy to live and grow. Energy moves through each community from producers to consumers. Some energy is passed along, but most is used as it flows through the ecosystem.

Critical Thinking

1. How does energy flow from a consumer to a decomposer to a producer?

2. If smoke blocked the sun for a long time, how would food chains be affected?

3. Why should it matter to you if a plant or an insect you've never heard of is endangered?

Staying In Balance

What do these animals need to stay alive? How do they get these things? In this lesson look for the different ways living things in a community act on each other to get what they need and keep their ecosystem in balance.

Minds On! What do you think would happen if zebras ate all the plants in their habitat? What would happen to other plant eaters? And what about the lions? They don't eat plants, but soon they wouldn't have any food, either. The whole ecosystem would be out of balance. Write your thoughts on page 17 of your *Activity Log.* ●

Gazelles, zebras, giraffe, and gemsbok at a waterhole at Etosha, Namibia

In the next activity, you will explore one of the ways organisms act on each other in order to survive (sər vīv´) in a habitat.

Activity!

Elbow Room!

You know that space is one of the needs of living things. You probably know what happens when there are too many people in one place. But what about plants? What happens when there are too many plants in one place? Does the amount of available space affect the way plants grow?

What You Need

Activity Log, pages 18-19

measuring cup   water

scissors

masking tape

meter tape

index cards   marker

soil from a yard or garden

seeds

4 milk cartons

What To Do

1 Cut the tops from the milk cartons. Label one A, one B, one C, and the last D. Carefully punch three drainage holes in the bottom of each carton. *Safety Tip:* Use scissors carefully.

2 Fill each carton to the same level with soil.

Safety!

See the *Safety Tip* in step 1.

3 Place 3 bean seeds, 3 corn seeds and 3 wheat seeds on top of the soil in carton A. Carefully sprinkle about 5 mm of soil over the seeds.

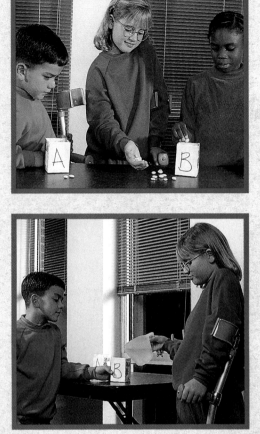

4 In the same way, plant 3 bean seeds in carton B. Plant 3 corn seeds in carton C. Plant 3 wheat seeds in carton D.

5 Place the cartons in a well lighted area. Predict what you think will happen by drawing what you think the plants will look like in 14 days.

6 Water the seeds every two days when the soil begins to dry out. Keep the soil moist, but do not overwater. Use the same amount of water for each carton. Observe the seeds for 2 weeks.

7 Record your observations on the chart in your *Activity Log.*

What Happened?

1. After 14 days, how many plants were there in each carton?
2. After 14 days, how did the plants in carton A compare in height to the plants in other cartons?
3. After 14 days, which type of plant seemed to be doing better?

What Now?

1. For what things were the plants in each carton competing?
2. How did the number of plants in carton A affect each plant getting what it needs?
3. How could you test how much space animals need?

EXPLORE

39

Competition

The number of plants in an area affects how they live and grow. The plants in cartons B, C, and D had larger leaves and were healthier. Each had more space, water, and soil than the carton A plants. The plants in carton A were more crowded. Less soil, water, and space affected their health.

When there are many organisms in an ecosystem, they are in competition for what they need to stay alive. **Competition** (kom´ pi tish´ ən) happens when one organism works against another to get something it needs to live. Most often, they compete for food. But even with plenty of food, the number of organisms in an area is limited by disease, space, and other things.

How many organisms can live in an ecosystem? It depends partly on the amount of rain, soil, and sunlight available for producers. Fewer plants can grow in a dry desert ecosystem. So fewer consumers can live in the desert.

Death Valley California

Rain forest in Equador

In a rain forest ecosystem, many plants can grow because there is plenty of rain, sunlight, and soil. Producers have enough energy to feed many consumers.

Gazelles

In each community, members of the same population compete because they eat the same things and live in the same habitat. For example, zebras compete with each other for food.

Members of different populations compete with each other for food, too. Lions and leopards both eat zebras, wildebeest (wil´də bēst´), and gazelles (gə zelz´). Lions and leopards are predators. A **predator** (pred´ə tər) is an animal that captures other animals for food. The animals that are eaten by a predator are called **prey** (prā).

Praying mantis eating copper butterfly

Some birds, insects, and fish are predators. Hawks and owls eat rabbits and mice. A praying mantis eats hundreds of other insects. Sharks and bass eat other fish. Predators can also become prey. Some birds eat praying mantises. Smaller fish are eaten by larger fish.

Cheetah

Avoiding Competition

Competition does take place, but populations avoid it because the goal of all living things is to survive. Avoiding competition makes it possible for more organisms to stay alive. How do organisms avoid competition?

They do it by being limited to a very particular behavior or food, which gives them their own place in the ecosystem. This place is their niche. A **niche** (nich) is the organism's job or role in the ecosystem. By being limited in this way, many different populations of organisms can share the same space, food, water, and other things they need to stay alive.

Consumers like zebras, wildebeest, and gazelles graze in the same area. They eat different parts of the grasses.

Zebra

Predators that hunt in different places at different times don't compete.

Predators also use different ways to capture their prey. Cheetahs use speed, leopards use ambush, and lions often bully another predator out of what it has killed and take the food for themselves.

Lions with Prey

42

These same behaviors can be seen in birds, insects, and other animals.

Three different kinds of tiny organisms called mites (mītz) live on three different areas of a honey bee's body.

Barn owl
Hawks and owls have the same prey, but they hunt at different times.

Twenty different insects use the North American white pine for food. They just eat different parts of the tree.

Adjusting in order to survive is also seen in plants. Each kind of plant has its own special place, or niche, which allows it to live and grow in its habitat.

Some grow in the early part of the growing season. Others grow later in the season.

California forest

North American pine
Some live in shade while others live in sunlight. Some live in moist soil. Others live in drier soil.

Cooperation

Besides avoiding competition, there is much cooperation among organisms. **Cooperation** happens when one organism is helpful in some way to another. Sometimes it occurs within a population.

There are many examples of cooperation between populations, too. Do you know of any plants that grow on other plants? What are some animals that use plants for shelter?

Some populations live in a close cooperative relationship called **symbiosis** (sim´ bē ō´ sis). In one kind of symbiosis, both populations are helped by living together.

Herds of elephants live together and protect each other. Fish swim together in a school for protection. Bees live in hives in which each bee has a responsibility.

In the ocean, 42 kinds of fish get their food by going inside the mouths of larger fish and cleaning the larger fish's teeth! The tiny fish get their food in this way.

Sweetlips with cleaner wrasse removing parasites

In another kind of symbiosis, only one of the populations is helped. Fish called remoras (rem´ ər əz) hitchhike rides on manta rays in the ocean.

There is also a kind of relationship in which one population is a parasite. A **parasite** (par´ ə sīt´) lives in or on another organism, called a **host.** A parasite is harmful to the host in some way.

Mistletoe is a parasite. This plant lives on trees and takes nutrients and water from them.

TRY THIS

Activity!

What's on That Leaf?

In this activity you will observe a parasite that lives in a gall. A **gall** is an unusual growth or swelling on a plant that can be caused by insects.

What You Need
jar, cheesecloth, rubber band, leaves with plant galls, *Activity Log* **page 20**

Place the leaves in the jar. Cover the top of the jar with cheesecloth. Hold it in place with the rubber band. Observe the galls. Record your observations. What stage of insect emerged from the gall? What stage of insect lives in a gall?

Your World in Balance

Relationships among organisms are happening all around you in yards, vacant lots, and parks.

Minds On! What predator/prey relationships do you see in this picture? What about cooperative relationships? What other examples of these relationships could you show by changing the picture? ●

Whether a habitat is large or small, the populations interact. What you've learned in this lesson will help you see more of what was going on in the Explore Activity on pages 14 and 15.

TRY THIS
Activity!

Revisit Your Ecosystem

In this activity you will identify the interactions of populations in a small ecosystem.

What You Need
Activity Log pages 4–5, page 21

Work in the same groups as in the Explore Activity. Read over your notes, and look at your drawing of the ecosystem. List examples of competition, ways of avoiding competition, and examples of cooperation among the populations. Compare your findings with those of other groups.

Music/Art  Link
Your Own Garden

Now that you know more about how populations interact with each other, plan and draw a garden on page 22 of your **Activity Log.** Include your favorite fruits, vegetables, and flowers. Use seed catalogs to find out what the plants you chose will need. The amount of light, water, and space as well as the kind of soil are all important. Finish by drawing any animals that would help your garden grow. Which ones would you like to stay away? Why?

Sum It Up

Balance in an ecosystem happens because populations interact to survive. Competition and cooperation are part of how this happens. Each population has a niche. That's part of it, too. There are changes and adjustments in the process. But over time, these interactions keep things balanced.

Critical Thinking

1. Remember the zebras? What two things might limit their population so they wouldn't eat all the grass in their habitat?

2. Squirrels and caterpillars live in the same habitat, but they don't compete. Why?

3. What's a predator for squirrels? For caterpillars?

Earth's Cycles

Water—you probably know you can't live without it. Other living things can't either. In this lesson you'll learn about some ways that water, oxygen, and other materials in an ecosystem are used over and over so we don't run out.

Tropical rain forest

Minds On! When rain sinks into the ground, what happens to it? Is it wasted? Should we try to save it? Draw a picture that shows what you think happens to rainwater on page 23 of your ***Activity Log.*** ●

48

Water is important to different living things in different ways. Some drink it. Others live in it. In the next activity, you'll explore how living things get what they need in a water habitat.

Activity!

You Can Make an Ecosystem

You probably know how much work it is to take care of a pet. Even plants need some care. Have you thought about how all the animals and plants in nature get what they need to live and grow? In this activity you will see how some of these materials are used over and over in an ecosystem.

What You Need

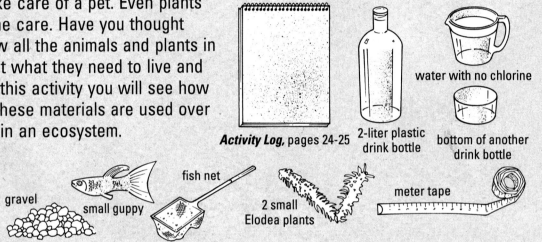

Activity Log, pages 24-25

2-liter plastic drink bottle

water with no chlorine

bottom of another drink bottle

fish food

gravel

small guppy

fish net

2 small Elodea plants

meter tape

What To Do

1 Wash the gravel until the water is clear. Put a layer of gravel about 3 cm deep in the bottom of the bottle your teacher will give you.

2 Fill the bottle about half full of water. Anchor the plants by gently pushing the roots into the gravel. Cover the bottle with part of another bottle that your teacher will give you. Put your ecosystem in a place where it receives plenty of light, but is not directly in the sun.

50

3 After 2 days, use the fish net to gently place the guppy in the bottle. Add one flake of fish food to the water in the bottle through one of the holes in the top. Later in the week, add another flake.

4 Observe this ecosystem for a period of 4 weeks, adding one flake of fish food twice each week. Record your observations in your *Activity Log.*

What Happened?

1. What does your ecosystem look like now compared to when you started? What does that tell you about how balanced your ecosystem is?

2. What did the fish need to survive?

3. What did the plant need to survive?

What Now?

1. What did the animal give to the ecosystem? What did the plants give to the ecosystem?

2. What did the light provide to the ecosystem? What did the water provide to the ecosystem?

3. How do you know that the living things are getting what they need?

EXPLORE

51

Cycles of Life

The ecosystem in the Explore Activity had two populations. Each used some of what the other put into the water. The plants used carbon dioxide and waste materials from the fish, energy from the sun, and oxygen to make food. They also produced oxygen. The guppy got energy from the fish food. It used oxygen from the plants. The plants also used some oxygen and produced some carbon dioxide as they used food. These exchanges between the fish and the plants happened over and over. As long as they continue, the ecosystem will be balanced.

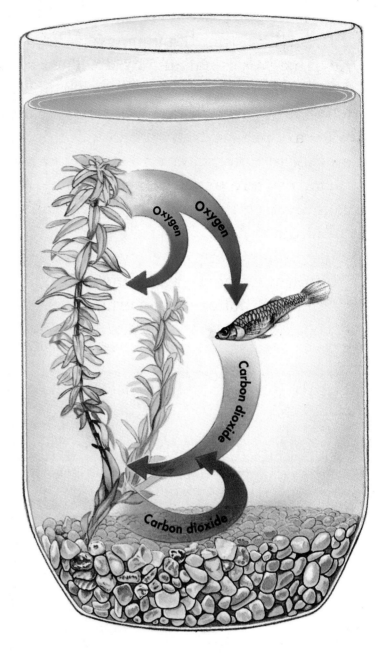

Literature 📖 Link

Very Last First Time

Fish get oxygen from water. You get it from air. Read *Very Last First Time* by Jan Andrews to find out about the water habitat that Eva visited when she walked on the bottom of the sea. On page 26 of your **Activity Log,** list the populations she saw. Choose one and find out more about it. Share what you learn with your class.

Something that happens over and over in the same way is called a **cycle**. The **carbon dioxide and oxygen cycle** is an exchange between producers and consumers. These gases are passed from one population to another in both water and land habitats. If the gases were used up instead of being exchanged in this cycle, the living things would die.

Earth has many other cycles. The seasons occur every year. Day and night happen every 24 hours. What are some other cycles?

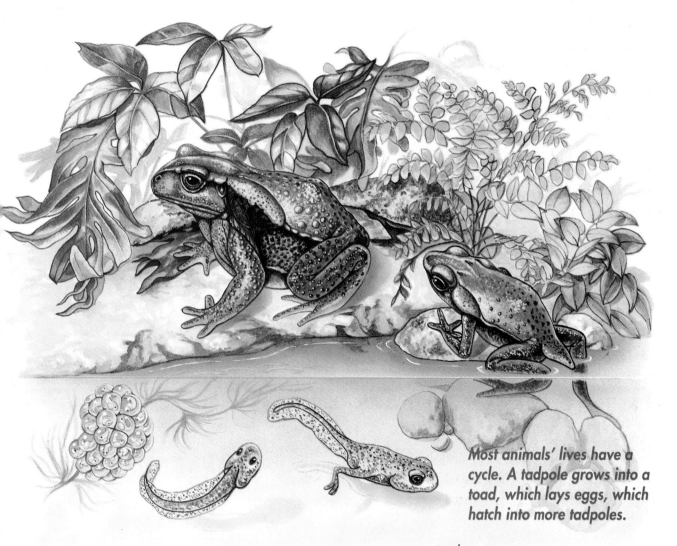

Most animals' lives have a cycle. A tadpole grows into a toad, which lays eggs, which hatch into more tadpoles.

The Water Cycle

Another important cycle in an ecosystem is the water cycle. The **water cycle** is the process by which water changes from solid to liquid to gas and back again. It is very important to living things. Look back at the picture you drew on page 23 of your *Activity Log* to show what you think happens to rainwater that sinks into the ground. How do your ideas match up with this diagram?

All living things need water. Green plants use water to make food. Some animals drink water. Others live in it.

What happens to water that falls to Earth? Some water runs along the ground and into oceans, lakes, rivers, and streams.

Some water sinks into the ground. It is called groundwater. Later, it flows into the lakes, rivers, and oceans on Earth's surface.

In the air, water vapor changes back into liquid water. It returns to Earth as dew, frost, rain, snow, sleet, or hail.

Water not used by green plants evaporates from their leaves and returns to the air. Some animals exhale (eks hāl´) water vapor as they breathe.

Activity!

Water While You Wait

You can make a model to show how part of the water cycle works.

What You Need

jar, water, measuring cup, plastic wrap, rubber band, *Activity Log* page 27

Put ½ cup of water in the jar. Cover the top with plastic wrap. Hold it in place with the rubber band. Put the jar in direct sunlight. Observe over three days. Record your observations. What part of the water cycle did you observe in this activity?

Water evaporates from surface water and the land and becomes water vapor.

Recycling

Everything is made of matter. The same matter that's on Earth now was here when the dinosaurs lived. It can't be destroyed or used up.

Earth recycles matter. **Recycle** means to change something that has been used into something that can be used again. As matter is recycled, it may change form several times.

Producers, like the corn plant, and consumers, like you, as well as scavengers and decomposers, take part in the recycling of matter.

When you eat corn, part of it becomes the cells in your body. The matter in the corn isn't gone. It just has a different form.

Taking Care of Earth

All living things, including you, need Earth's natural resources. A **natural resource** is a material found in nature that is useful or necessary to living things. Water, oxygen, trees, and minerals are examples of natural resources.

You have learned that some of Earth's resources are recycled through the actions of living things. But sometimes people interfere. For example, we do things to change the oxygen and carbon dioxide cycle.

Destroying large parts of Earth's rain forests can lead to more carbon dioxide and less oxygen in the air.

Destruction of tropical rain forest in Costa Rica

Polluting the oceans kills algae (al´jē) and other organisms that produce much of Earth's oxygen.

Tanker spilling oil into ocean

If we stop doing these things, Earth will be better able to keep this important cycle in balance.

Trouble Here!

With a small group, find places where ecosystems are in trouble. For example, parts of North America are being harmed by acid rain. In South America, rain forests are being cut and burned. Fishing areas in Asia have been polluted. Design IN TROUBLE symbols, and mark these places on a map. Have each person tell the class about one area. Pretend to be "on the scene" TV reporters. Be sure to tell what is being done to solve the problem.

One problem we can all work on is saving trees. We can stop wasting paper. We can recycle the paper we use. And we can buy products that have been made with recycled materials.

Where is the recycling center closest to where you live? What materials do they accept?

Activity!

Use It Up!

In this activity you'll work in groups to save and recycle your class's waste paper.

What You Need

2 cardboard boxes, *Activity Log* **page 28**

Separate waste paper that your group has used into two stacks each day. Put completely used paper into one box. Put reusable paper into the other box. After 5 days, compare the amounts in the boxes. List ways that your reusable paper could be used again. How could your group have used less paper? Compare your ideas with those of other groups. Take the completely used paper to a recycling center.

Sum It Up

Earth supplies what living things need. These materials are used and reused by different organisms at different times. As the living and nonliving things in an ecosystem interact, these cycles occur. When they are interrupted, the ecosystem becomes unbalanced.

Critical Thinking

1. People sometimes change matter into a form that can't be used again. What's one example?

2. How does the change in seasons help Earth recycle its resources?

3. Do people have a life cycle? What is it?

59

What Can You Do?

You have learned to think of Earth as an ecosystem. All living and nonliving things are part of it. When humans damage the ecosystem, the living things are affected. The nonliving things are affected, too. Taking care of Earth is a big job. None of us can do it alone. Here are some things you can do to help.

In Your Home

- Save glass jars and bottles, newspapers, and aluminum cans. With your parents, take them to a recycling center.

- Save plastic bags to line wastebaskets.

Recycling center in Edison, N.J.

TRY THIS Activity!

Fill It Up

You can make containers to collect materials you want to recycle.

What You Need

3 strong cardboard boxes, marker, *Activity Log* page 29

Label each box with what it will hold. Mark them NEWSPAPERS, GLASS, and CANS. Draw pictures on them, if you want to. Ask your family to help by putting things in the right box. Use the boxes to take what you collect to the nearest recycling center. How much did your family collect? What are some other ways to reduce the amount of trash you produce? Write your thoughts in your ***Activity Log.***

When You Shop

- Practice precycling. **Precycling** (prē sī´kling) means buying wisely so there is less to recycle. Ask your family not to buy things with too much packaging or wrapping. Some of packaging keeps things clean and safe. But too much is wasteful.

- Take your own grocery bags to the store with you. Use them until they wear out.

- Ask your family to buy cleaners that are biodegradable. **Biodegradable** (bī´ō di grā´də bəl) means capable of being decayed naturally. Materials that aren't biodegradable can poison the soil and water. Read the labels. Look for the words *biodegradable* and *degradable* on the things you buy.

TRY THIS Activity!

Enough Is Enough!

What kinds of packaging make sense? What kinds are wasteful? In this activity you'll observe and evaluate the packaging of products.

What You Need
Activity Log page 30

Look in the refrigerator and the cabinets in your home. Observe the way products are packaged. Are there any that are covered in unnecessary cardboard or plastic? Record what you observe. Now visit a supermarket. Find examples of enough packaging and too much packaging. Look at products such as deodorants and cleaners, as well as food. Record your observations. Compare them with those of other students.

10 Trash bags

fits up to 30 gallon can

DEGRADABLE
ACTIVATED BY EXPOSURE TO THE ELEMENTS

For the Animals

● Cut apart the plastic rings that connect some aluminum cans. Animals can get tangled in them.

● Plant flowers like marigolds or sweet william. Butterflies are attracted to these plants.

● Help the birds build their nests in the spring.

Gull caught in plastic rings

TRY THIS

Activity!

New Housing

How can recycling help the birds? They can use what you collect to build their nests.

What You Need
net bag, small sticks, string, hair from a hairbrush, lint from a dryer, scissors, *Activity Log* page 31

Fill the net bag with hair, sticks, lint, and cut-up bits of string. Be sure everything is in small pieces. Tie the bag shut. Pull some of the materials part way through the net. Use string to tie the bag to a branch of a tree. Observe the bag over the next four weeks. Record your observations.

Biosphere II is a miniature Earth.

Habitat for humans

Farm

An Experiment in Living

In the desert near Tucson, Arizona, eight people have an idea for taking care of Earth. They are living inside a glass and steel dome called Biosphere II (bī´ə sfîr´). They are trying to find the right mixture of plants and animals that will allow an artificial ecosystem to supply all of its own needs.

Will they be successful? No one knows. If the carbon dioxide and oxygen cycle or the water cycle becomes unbalanced, the experiment will be over. But if the ecosystem works, we'll learn how to take better care of Biosphere I—Earth. And that will be very good news for us all.

SCIENCE
TECHNOLOGY
AND
Society

Focus
on
Technology

Biosphere II has its own water and air.

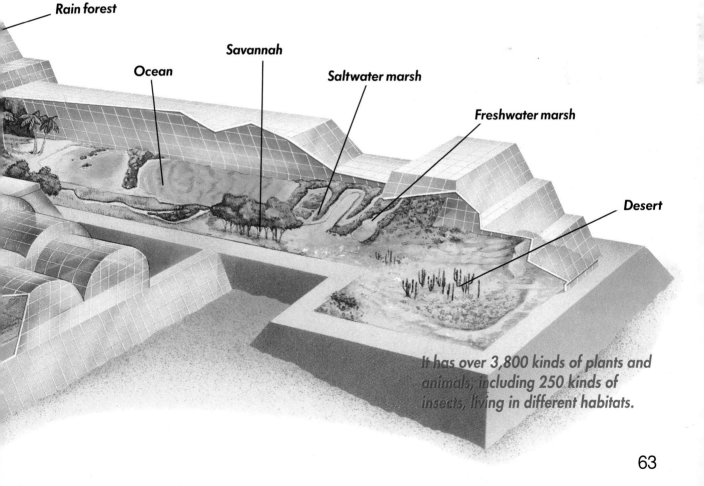

Rain forest

Savannah

Ocean

Saltwater marsh

Freshwater marsh

Desert

It has over 3,800 kinds of plants and animals, including 250 kinds of insects, living in different habitats.

63

GLOSSARY

Use the pronunciation key below to help you decode, or read, the pronunciations.

Pronunciation Key

a	at, bad	d	dear, soda, bad
ā	ape, pain, day, break	f	five, defend, leaf, off, cough, elephant
ä	father, car, heart	g	game, ago, fog, egg
âr	care, pair, bear, their, where	h	hat, ahead
e	end, pet, said, heaven, friend	hw	white, whether, which
ē	equal, me, feet, team, piece, key	j	joke, enjoy, gem, page, edge
i	it, big, English, hymn	k	kite, bakery, seek, tack, cat
ī	ice, fine, lie, my	l	lid, sailor, feel, ball, allow
îr	ear, deer, here, pierce	m	man, family, dream
o	odd, hot, watch	n	not, final, pan, knife
ō	old, oat, toe, low	ng	long, singer, pink
ô	coffee, all, taught, law, fought	p	pail, repair, soap, happy
ôr	order, fork, horse, story, pour	r	ride, parent, wear, more, marry
oi	oil, toy	s	sit, aside, pets, cent, pass
ou	out, now	sh	shoe, washer, fish mission, nation
u	up, mud, love, double	t	tag, pretend, fat, button, dressed
ū	use, mule, cue, feud, few	th	thin, panther, both
ü	rule, true, food	th	this, mother, smooth
ú	put, wood, should	v	very, favor, wave
ûr	burn, hurry, term, bird, word, courage	w	wet, weather, reward
ə	about, taken, pencil, lemon, circus	y	yes, onion
b	bat, above, job	z	zoo, lazy, jazz, rose, dogs, houses
ch	chin, such, match	zh	vision, treasure, seizure

bacteria (bak tîr´ē ə) one-celled organisms that are so small that they can be seen only through a microscope. Bacteria are found in air, soil, and water, and in and on all plants and animals.

biodegradable (bī´ō di grā´də bəl) capable of being decayed naturally

carbon dioxide (kär´bon dī ok´sīd) a colorless, odorless gas, made up of carbon and oxygen, that is present in the atmosphere. Carbon dioxide is exhaled by animals as a waste product and used by plants to make food.

carbon dioxide and oxygen cycle— the movement of two gases through Earth's ecosystems as they are exchanged by producers and consumers

community (kə mū´ ni tē) all the animals, plants, and other organisms that live in a certain area and interact with each other

competition (kom´pi tish´ən) the active seeking after and use of a resource that is in limited supply by two or more organisms. For example, animals compete for food, and plants compete for light, water, and space.

compost (kom´pōst) a mixture of decaying plant materials that makes soil richer and more fertile

consumer (kən sü´mər) an organism that can't make its own food. A consumer uses other organisms for food.

cooperation (kō op´ə rā´shən) the act of one organism getting a benefit from another in a non-harmful way. For example, trees provide shelter for animals, as well as a place for other plants such as vines to grow.

cycle (sī´kəl) a series of events or actions that happens over and over in the same way

decomposer (dē´kəm pō´zər) an organism that gets food by breaking down dead plant and animal matter into simpler substances. For example, fungi and some bacteria are decomposers.

ecosystem (ek´ō sis´təm) a system in which all the living things in a community interact with each other and the place where they live

endangered (en dān´jərd) having very few living members. An endangered organism is in danger of becoming extinct.

extinct (ek stingkt´) having no living members. When there are no more of a particular plant or animal still alive, it is extinct.

food chain system in which each plant, animal, or other organism in the sequence feeds upon the one below it. An example of a food chain is plant–plant louse–ladybug–spider–small bird–hawk. Each dash in the food chain means "is eaten by."

food web overlapping food chains in a community

fungi (fun´jī) organisms, such as molds, yeasts, and mushrooms that get food by causing dead organisms to decay

gall an unusual growth or swelling on the leaves, stems, or roots of a plant that can be caused by insects, bacteria, or fungi

habitat (hab´i tat´) the place in an ecosystem where a population lives

host (hōst) the organism a parasite lives in or on

mineral (min´ər əl) a nonliving solid found in nature but not made by plants or animals. Organisms need small amounts of certain minerals to survive.

natural resource—material found in nature that is useful or necessary to living things. Air and water are examples of natural resources.

nematode (nem´ə tōd) a small worm that is round with pointed ends. Some nematodes are parasites, but others are not.

niche (nich) an organism's job or role in the ecosystem

organism (ôr´gə niz´əm) a living thing

oxygen (ok´sə jən) a colorless, tasteless, and odorless gas found in air that is necessary for life

parasite (par´ə sīt´) a living thing

that lives in or on another living thing, taking something from it such as food or water

population (pop´yə lā´shən) a group of the same kind of organisms living in the same place

precycling (prē sī´kling) the process of buying wisely so there is less to recycle. Avoiding products with wasteful packaging is an example of precycling.

predator (pred´ə tər) an animal that kills other animals for food

prey (prā) an animal that is eaten by a predator

producer (prə dü´sər) an organism that uses energy in sunlight to make its own food

recycle (rē sī´kəl) the process of changing something that has been used into something that can be used again

scavenger (skav´ən jər) an animal that gets food by eating dead plants or animals

survive (sər vīv´) to continue to live and stay active

symbiosis (sim´bē ō´sis) a close, cooperative relationship between two different kinds of organisms

water cycle the process by which water changes from solid to liquid to gas and back again. Plants and animals take part in the water cycle by adding water vapor to air.

INDEX

CREDITS